Contents

VILLAGE FROM ABOVE

Villages are found in the countryside all over Britain. Most towns and cities began as villages, and slowly got bigger and bigger! Like towns and cities, villages are shown on maps.

Learning to read maps will help you to explore villages and the countryside.

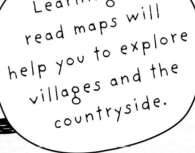

What are maps?

Maps are drawings of the landscape seen from above, like a bird's eye view. We use maps to find out where things are and make journeys. Most maps have a title, which explains what the map shows.

This page shows a photo and a map of the same village.

The map shows things more simply, so important features are easier to see.

Photo of a village in the Cotswolds

This photo shows a village from above. It was taken from a plane.

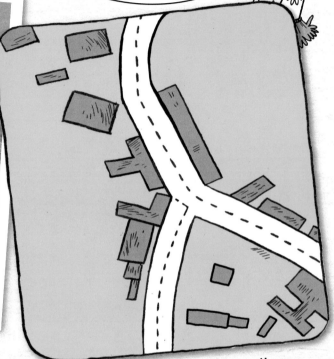

This map shows the same village. Compare it with the photo.

TRY THIS!

To make a map you need to imagine what things look like from above, as if you were a bird flying over the landscape. Practise this skill by drawing a map of this house as if you were looking from directly above.

5

VILLAGE LANDMARKS

A landmark is a feature that you can see clearly, such as a church with a steeple. Landmarks help you find your way around a village. Landmarks in the village shown below include a school, a church and a car park.

This map has drawings of features in the village.

KEY

✝ Church

SCH School

P Parking

This map has symbols. The key explains what the symbols mean.

Map symbols

Landmarks are shown on most maps as signs, or symbols. Map symbols can be letters, such as P for Parking. Or they can be very simple drawings, such as a little flag to show a golf course. Roads and railways are shown as lines. Coloured areas mark lakes and woodlands.

The key at the side explains what the symbols mean.

KEY
PO Post Office
📖 Library
⚐ Golf course

TRY THIS!

This map shows another village with different landmarks. Look at the map and the key, and answer these questions:

- Does the village have a post office?
- Is there a library?
- Can you see a church?

A VILLAGE TO DIFFERENT SCALES

All maps show things smaller than they really are. Everything on the map is drawn to the same size. This is called the scale.

Different scales

The scale bar at the bottom of the map gives the scale.

0   0.1   0.2   0.3   0.4   0.5   km

Maps are drawn to different scales. The map above shows just the centre of a small village. This small area is shown in a lot of detail. The map opposite shows the same village and the surrounding countryside.

This larger area is shown in less detail. Other maps show an even larger area, such as a whole region, a country such as Britain, or even the world.

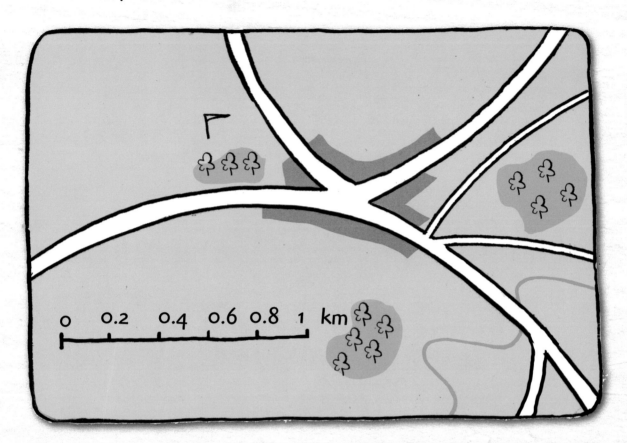

TRY THIS!

Maps of different scales are useful in different ways.

- Which of these two maps would you use to find your way around the village?
- Which one would you use to go for a country walk?

USING SCALE ON THE COMMON

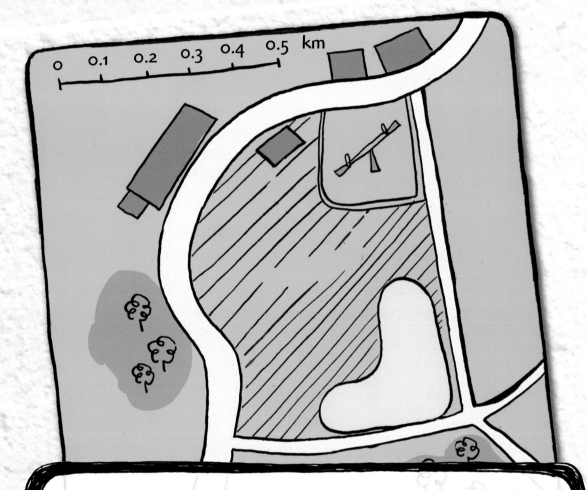

Scale and distance

A map's scale allows you to work out the actual distance on the ground. The scale bar gives the distance in centimetres or inches, and also in miles or kilometres. Look at this map of a village common. On this large-scale map, 1 centimetre represents 100 metres, so 10 centimetres represents 1 kilometre.

How far?

Knowing the distance between places can help you to work out roughly how long it will take to walk.

If you walk fast, you can cover 4 kilometres in an hour – that's 1 kilometre every 15 minutes.

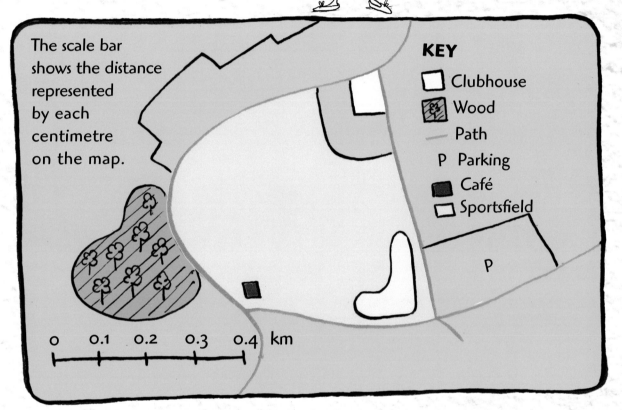

The scale bar shows the distance represented by each centimetre on the map.

KEY
- Clubhouse
- Wood
- Path
- P Parking
- Café
- Sportsfield

0   0.1   0.2   0.3   0.4   km

TRY THIS!

Use a ruler to measure the distance between the clubhouse and the café. Now place the ruler along the scale bar to work out the distance in kilometres. How long do you think it would take you to walk?

FROM SCHOOL TO SWIMMING POOL

Maps show the location of important buildings in a village. This helps you to work out how near or far away places are.

Looking at the map tells you whether to turn right, left or go straight on to walk from one place to another.

Places on a street map

Street maps are large-scale maps that show the names of streets. The street map opposite shows a village with a school and a swimming pool. Once a week, each class visits the pool for a swimming lesson.

Street maps show you how to get from one place to another. Look at the map. Miss Brown's class usually walks along Rambling Road. They then cross the street to reach Pool Lane and the swimming pool. Follow the route on the map.

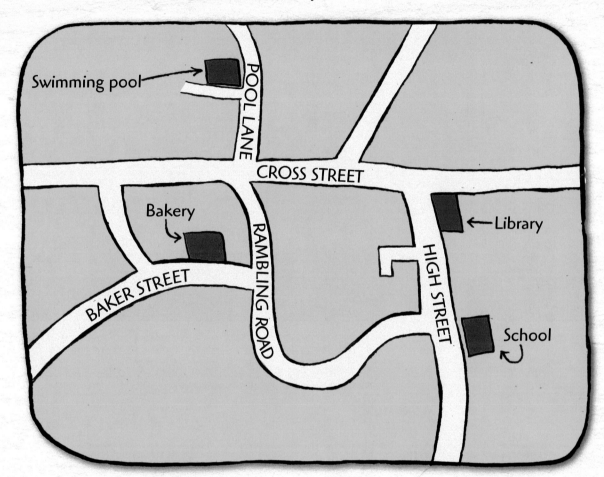

TRY THIS!

Have another look at the map. Can you see a quicker way to get from the school to the swimming pool? Write down the directions to give the teacher. Mention any landmarks you pass.

PLAN OF A VILLAGE SHOP

Some villages have many shops, such as a bakery, a grocery store and a chemist.

Most villages have at least one shop, which may be a post office and supermarket rolled into one.

Plan maps

Plans are very large-scale maps that show a building such as a shop in a lot of detail. They may show furniture and features such as doors and windows. Architects draw plans when they design buildings. Shopkeepers use plans to decide how to arrange the shop.

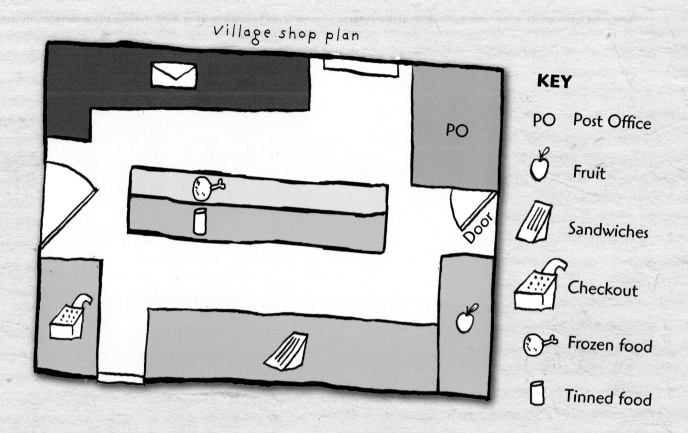

Village shop plan

KEY

PO — Post Office

Fruit

Sandwiches

Checkout

Frozen food

Tinned food

TRY THIS!

Make a plan of a small shop or your bedroom. First use a ruler to measure the length of your foot. Then pace the length and width of the room, counting the number of footsteps. Multiply by your foot measurement to find the dimensions of the room. Draw the room on squared paper. Measure furniture such as shop counters in the same way, and mark them on the plan.

If you choose a shop, you need to ask the owner's permission!

A TRIP TO THE MARKET

Farmers' markets take place in many villages on a Saturday.

Farmers set up little stalls to sell their produce. Each farmer has a different stall.

A plan can help you find your way around a busy market like this one.

Stall plan

Plan maps can show the location of temporary features such as stalls at a market. Market planners use these maps to make sure there is enough room for everyone!

The plan may be displayed at the entrance, so shoppers can use it to locate their favourite stalls. They can also use it to plan their route.

CHEESE
FISH
BREAD
MEAT
BANANAS
CAKES

Plan of Saturday market

TRY THIS!

Imagine you are visiting the market to buy your shopping. Look at the shopping list and the plan of the market. Plan the quickest route to tick off all the things on your list.

HOW A COMPASS WORKS

COMPASS POINTS AT THE STABLES

A compass is a vital tool that tells you which way you are going. A compass can also help you locate places and follow directions on a map.

All compasses have a magnetic needle, which always points north.

You can use this to work out the four main compass directions: north, south, east and west.

Many maps have a compass rose that shows which way is north. On most maps, north is shown at the top.

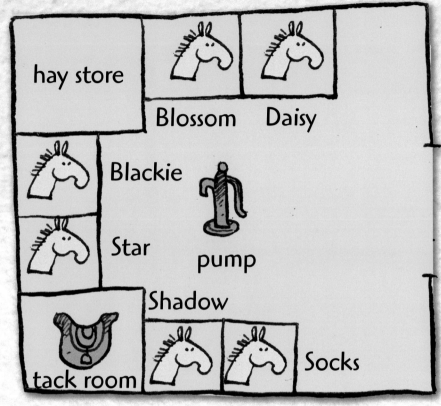

This compass rose shows four points between the main directions: northeast (NE), southeast (SE), southwest (SW) and northwest (NW).

TRY THIS!

A compass rose allows you to give and follow directions to find the exact location of places. For example, on this map of a stable yard, Blossom's stable lies due north of the pump in the centre. Look at the map and answer these questions:

- In which direction would you walk to take water from the pump to Socks?
- In which direction would you walk to give Daisy hay from the hay store?

A COUNTRY WALK

If you go for a country walk, you will need a map to plan your route, and follow it on the ground. Symbols on the map show local landmarks. The map below shows some new map symbols.

KEY
- ······· Footpath
- – – – Bridleway
- Caravan site
- Nature reserve

Footpaths and bridleways

Paths link villages. They allow everyone to enjoy the countryside. There are two main types of paths: footpaths and bridleways. They are shown on maps with different symbols.

Footpaths are for walkers only. Horse-riders, cyclists and walkers can use bridleways.

TRY THIS!

Make a map of your favourite walk from memory. Use symbols to mark the landmarks you pass. You may need to make up your own symbols. Show your route as a dotted line. Now check your memory map against a real map of the same area.

GRID ON THE GREEN

Some villages have a green in the centre, with houses around it. This map of a village green has lines running up and down, and across the page.

The lines form a grid of squares, which you can use to locate places exactly.

KEY

Buildings

Village green

Church

Campsite

Windmill

Grid references

Look at the sides of the map. The squares running across the page have letters. The squares running up the page have numbers. The letters and numbers provide an exact location, called a grid reference.

Grid references are always read in a certain order.

Place your finger on the bottom left-hand corner of the map. Run your finger along the map, to read the east-west reference, shown by a letter. Then run your finger up the map to find the north-south reference, shown by a number.

TRY THIS!

Practise using grid references. Locate the church in square B1. Now answer these questions:

- What feature is shown in square A2?
- Give the grid reference for the windmill.

IN THE VALLEY

In hilly country most villages are found in valleys, which are lower than the surrounding land. But how can you show hills and valleys on the flat surface of a map?

Contour lines

The ups and downs of the landscape are shown on maps using lines called contours. These lines join places at the same height above sea level. Look at the map opposite of a village in a valley. Some of the lines have numbers, which give the height.

Numbers called spot heights mark the top of hills.

You can use contour lines to read the landscape. Numbers on the lines always face uphill, so you can see which way the land is sloping. Where contour lines are close together, the land slopes steeply. Where the lines are far apart, the land is fairly flat.

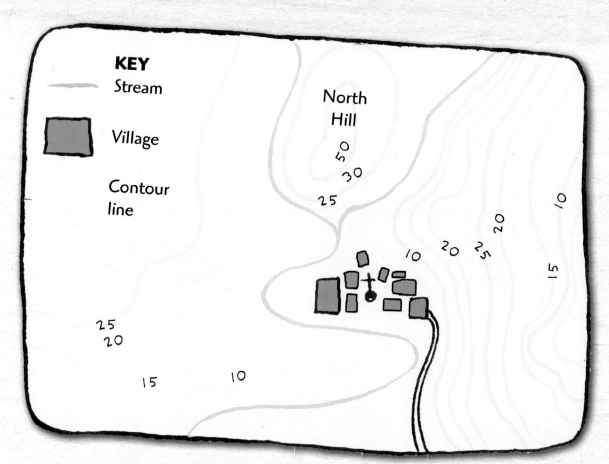

TRY THIS!

Look at the map and answer these questions:

- What height is the village?
- What is the highest point on the map?
- Where does the land slope most steeply?

LAND USE IN A VILLAGE

Not all maps tell you about the physical features of landscape. Some maps give other kinds of information, such as what the land is used for in a village. These are called land use maps.

Church

Doctors' surgery

Library

KEY
- Public building
- House
- Shop
- Office

Land use maps

Look at this land use map of a village. Buildings that are used in different ways are shown in different colours. For example, houses where people live are shown in blue and offices are shown in red.

The land use map below shows a farm on the edge of a village. The farmer grows crops and also keeps sheep and cows. He uses his fields in different ways each year. A field that is used to grow crops one year may grazed by sheep the next.

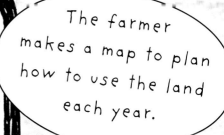

The farmer makes a map to plan how to use the land each year.

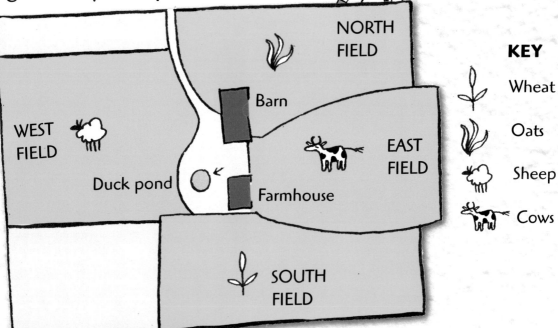

KEY

Wheat
Oats
Sheep
Cows

TRY THIS!

Look at the map and answer these questions:

- Which field is being used to grow wheat?
- What is going on in North Field?
- Name two fields that are being used for animals.

COUNTRY ROADS

Roads link villages in the countryside with nearby towns and cities. Narrow, winding lanes run between villages. A main road may lead to the nearest town. Nearby may be a motorway, which links towns and cities.

Different types of roads are shown in different colours on maps.

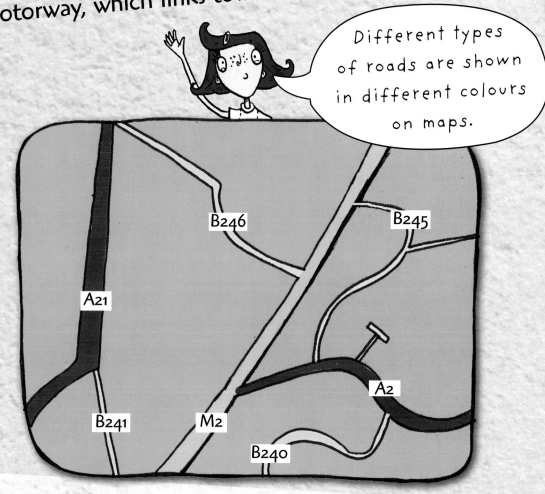

B246

B245

A21

A2

B241

M2

B240

Road maps

Road maps are used for journeys by car or bus. These maps show a large area, but only the roads are marked in detail. Villages and towns are shown as dots or coloured areas. These maps do not show what the landscape is like.

Bus maps

The map below shows bus routes in a country area. The roads are not shown accurately. Instead, the map shows the stops very clearly, so people using the bus know exactly where to get on and off.

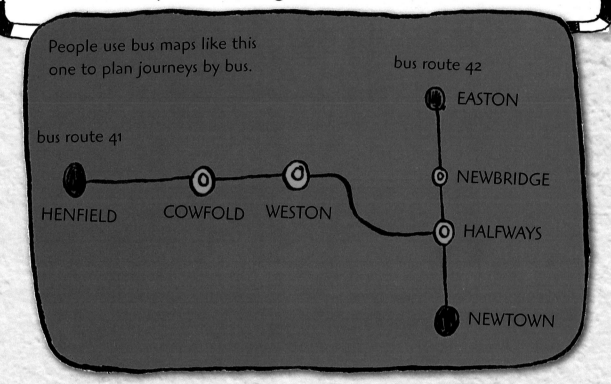

People use bus maps like this one to plan journeys by bus.

bus route 42

EASTON

bus route 41

HENFIELD   COWFOLD   WESTON

NEWBRIDGE

HALFWAYS

NEWTOWN

TRY THIS!

Look at the bus map and answer these questions:

- What bus would you take to get from Henfield to Weston?
- How would you get from Henfield to Newtown?

What the words mean

Bridleway A path that can be used by walkers, cyclists and horseriders.

Common A green space in or near a village. This public space may include a sportsfield and a playground.

Compass rose A symbol that shows compass directions.

Contour lines Lines on a map that show the height above sea level.

Grid Lines running across and down a map that divide the map into squares.

Grid reference Directions for a location provided by the grid on a map.

Key Panel on a map that shows the meaning of symbols.

Land use map A map that shows what land is used for.

Plan A large-scale map of a building or room.

Road map A small-scale map that shows roads.

Scale The size a map is drawn to.

Steeple A spire on a church, sometimes on a tower.

Street map A large-scale map showing street names.

Symbol A picture that stands for something else.

Temporary Of something which is not always there.

More information

Books

Marta Segal Block and Daniel R Block, *Reading Maps* (Heinemann, 2008)

Sally Hewitt, *Project Geography: Maps* (Franklin Watts, 2013)

Barbara Taylor, *Mapping Britain's Landscapes: Cities, Towns and Villages* (Franklin Watts, 2012)

Websites

Mapskills (PowerPoint) – Think Geography

www.thinkgeography.org.uk/Year%20 8%20Geog/.../Mapskills.ppt
This site explains map skills and has lots of exercises to practise your map skills.

Ordnance Survey: Map reading made easy

http://mapzone.ordnancesurvey.co.uk/ mapzone/PagesHomeworkHelp/docs/ easypeasy.pdf
Download this handy guide to map reading.

BBC – GCSE Bitesize: Basics of mapping: 1

www.bbc.co.uk/schools/gcsebitesize/ geography/geographical_skills/maps_ rev1.shtml
A summary of map reading skills for pupils learning geography at school.

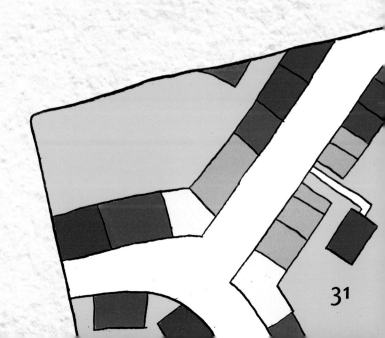

Index